The Black Fantasy Markets

Paula Whitney Best, MA, JD

An African American former corporation lawyer uses fantasy to teach young Black children *and their families* the difference between a stock and a bond, as well as the overall capital markets, on their way to generational wealth accumulation.

Copyright © 2024 Paula Whitney Best, MA, JD
All rights reserved
First Edition

NEWMAN SPRINGS PUBLISHING
320 Broad Street
Red Bank, NJ 07701

First originally published by Newman Springs Publishing 2024

ISBN 979-8-89061-152-9 (Paperback)
ISBN 979-8-89061-413-1 (Hardcover)
ISBN 979-8-89061-153-6 (Digital)

Printed in the United States of America

Dedicated to:

- My late wife, Victoria Soliwoda [so-lee-voh-dah]
- My late paternal grandmother, Lillian Lewis Best Coates
- My families
- My twenty-plus healthcare providers
- The A Better Chance (ABC) Program
- The Cambridge School of Weston, MA
- The Benjamin N. Cardozo School of Law at Yeshiva University, New York, NY
- Medgar Evers College of the City University of New York, Brooklyn, NY
- Chelsea Community Church, New York, NY

Common people can do uncommon things.

—Lisa Bluder, Retired Head Women's Basketball Coach, University of Iowa Hawkeyes, to Caitlin Clark, Basketball Player, during the 2023 NCAA Division 1 women's basketball championship tournament final game in their loss to Head Coach Kim Mulkey's LSU Tigers.[1]

---
[1] Both Confucius and George Washington Carver have stated variations on this theme.

Acknowledgments

Without the following people and institutions, this book would have been completely impossible:

- The late Prof. John L. Hanks for his vision, faith, and overall gambler's luck in securing me a seat in law school.
- Prof. David Gray Carlson, without whom I would not have become a published member of the *Cardozo Law Review*.
- John Pieper of Pieper Bar Review had an unshakable belief that I would pass both the New York and Connecticut bar examinations the second time around.
- My dad, along with my mother, raised five children in the New York City Lillian D. Wald public housing project on Manhattan's Lower East Side. All of us graduated from high school. My brother, Darryl H., and I earned college degrees. My sister, Laura Lillian, was a violoncello major at the prestigious Manhattan School of Music. Finally, my sisters, Janice C. and Leslie C., were charged with the most important job of all; they became amazing homemakers raising six wonderful children between them.
- My "Auntie" June Maud DeVonish Brown, gave me a room, food, and money to get through law school and my first attempt at the bar examinations.
- Alexander Pashkowsky, insisted that I dance to the Motown sound in my apartment as I studied relentlessly for the bar examinations redux.

- Gregory Murden, among so many other things, took me home from countless numbers of hospitalizations of which I have since lost track.
- Ellen K. Gronningen, a graduate of both the Juilliard and Manhattan Schools of Music, violinist, and my violin teacher par excellence. She played JS Bach to me as I spent eleven days on life support in the intensive care unit of a major New York City hospital.
- The New York City Summer Youth Employment Program (SYEP) and Laura P. James, Senior Director of SYEP at the Medgar Evers College of the City University of New York. She allowed me to cut my teeth on educating low-income, and students of color on the Capital Markets.
- AH, my 2019 SYEP graduate, I have known since she was seventeen years old, was my line spacing engineer. Without them, my manuscript might not have been accepted.
- The late great reverend Dr. Martin Luther King Jr. As an African-Caribbean American individual, nothing more needs to be said.
- Finally, the late, great, one and only Ella Fitzgerald for being the soundtrack of my law school years and beyond.

Foreword to the Families and Their Children

Good day! I do hope all is well.

Why you and your children should read my book.

If you are a Black or African American person with a child or children, you are likely to be a single parent.[2] Thus, you probably fall into one, if not all, of the following categories that measure wealth accumulation:

The racial wealth gap

This is something with which you are probably all too familiar. Wealth is simple. It is assets minus liabilities. In other words, it is what you own minus what you owe. This is likely to be a negative number. Thus, you probably have more bills than you have money with which to pay them. In 2016, White families had nearly ten times the net worth of Black families.[3] This is called the net worth gap. Thus, the total racial wealth gap is estimated at $10.14 trillion.[4]

The Brookings Institution is a think tank. This is an organization of people and groups that influence public policy. Do not be intimidated, but this affects you and your family daily.

---

[2] File: Nonmarital Birth Rates in the United States, 1940–2014. Data from Centers for Disease Control and Prevention, National Vital Statistics System Reports, 1.

[3] Vanessa Williamson, "Closing the Racial Wealth Gap Requires Heavy, Progressive Taxation of Wealth," *Brookings Blueprints for American Renewal and Prosperity Project*, Wednesday, December 9, 2020, https://www.brookings.edu/research/closing-the-racial-wealth-gap-requires-heavy-progressive-taxation-of-wealth/.

[4] Ibid.

The income gap

This is where it gets a little bit tricky. While White and Black people may earn the same income annually, Whites are better off than Black people due to prior White income and inheritances.[5] Black people are less likely to be recipients of inheritances due to the overall absence of Black generational wealth.

The homeownership gap

As you read my book, you will likely be a renter versus a homeowner. In 2017, there was a thirty-point gap between the two groups.[6]

These are the glaring Black/White wealth disparities that must be addressed if *anything* is to be changed. My book addresses a number of these highly charged complex social and economic issues, including race, gender, wealth, widowhood, loss of a mother, fatherhood, patents, bullying, imagination, creativity, entrepreneurship, a home fire, crime, and most of all, *making money*. If you do not wish for your sacred children to reach a similar fate of wealth disparities, please buy or borrow my book.

Many thanks in advance.

Paula Whitney Best, MA, JD

---

[5] John Bailey Jones and Urvi Neelakantan, "How Big Is the Inheritance Gap Between Black and White Families?" *Federal Reserve Bank of Richmond Economic Brief*, No. 22–49, December 2022, https://www.richmondfed.org/publications/research/economic_brief/2022/eb_22-49#:~:text=extremely%20large%20transfers.-,One%20of%20the%20most%20striking%20differences%20between%20Black%20and%20White,a%20large%20disparity%20in%20wealth.&text=The%20scale%20of%20the%20gap,counterpart%20(%24180%2C400%20versus%20%2420%2C700).

[6] Ana-Ioana Ciochia, "10+ Home Ownership Statistics and Facts for 2023. Homeownership by Race," Finmasters, Updated January 26, 2023, https://finmasters.com/home-ownership-statistics/?gclid=EAIaIQobChMIhNKNoOR_gIVAs7ICh0RegzmEAAYASAAEgJi1vD_BwE#Who-Are-American-Homeowners.

Come Meet the Characters in All Four Books!

- *Daddi (D)*; An African American forty-something-year-old responsible father of two precocious young children named *Stocki (S)*, girl, and *Bondi (B)*, boy, ages thirteen and ten, respectively. A blurred picture of *Mommi*, their late wife and mother, is prominently displayed on a nearby wall.
- *Madame Capital Market, a.k.a. Ma'am (M)*; a middle-aged Black woman. She is the home of *Corporation #1, Corpi #1, (C#1)*; a White European American man, *Corporation #2, Corpi #2, (C#2)*; a White European American woman, and *Corporation #3, Corpi #3, (C#3)*; a Black woman. They do magical things for the right price!
- *Mr. SECi, Principal A*; a White European American man; the Securities and Exchange Commission. He makes certain that Ma'am Capital Market and the Corpis do *not* take advantage of Daddi and his children, Stocki, and Bondi, when they invest in the Capital Markets.
- *Ms. Fedi, Principal B*; a Black woman; the Federal Reserve Bank. She makes certain that Madam Capital Market and the Corpis *behave* with Stocki and Bondi by managing LITTLE i's or INTEREST RATES; Little i's; race and gender neutral. *Interest Rates rule the world!*
- *Riskis (R)*; race and gender neutral; risks. Stock and bond buying involve Risks, which everybody needs to watch out for *before* investing.

- *Diversi (D)*; race and gender neutral; diversification. This Diversi, is everybody's *best* friend. Stocki and Bondi must be mindful *not* to place all of their eggs in one basket when buying stocks and bonds.
- *Evil Taxis (T)*; is a White European American man; taxes. Those are the Evil Taxes that everybody hates, particularly on *April fifteenth of most years.*

Next stop: a four-part journey into *making money.*

BOOK #1: ENTER THE FAMILY

During spring break on one warm sunny day in April 2023 on President Street between Bedford and Franklin Avenues in Crown Heights, Brooklyn, NY.

Daddi (D): Wake up, Stocki! Wake up, Bondi! It is time to get up! We have to get going! Good morning!

Stocki (S) and Bondi (B) together: Good morning, Daddi! Why?

S: There is no school today. We are on spring break! There is no school today.

D: Yes, I know! But we are going to a different type of school today.

S and B: Huh?

B: Why, Daddi?

D: Because I want to teach you something that is not being taught in your school today. At least not yet.

S: Are we going somewhere new?

B: Yes, Daddi, are we going somewhere new?

D: Yes, my darling motherless children. You and I are going to learn new things that will help you for the rest of our lives. I, too, will learn new things because I never learned this when I was your age (a picture of a blurred Mommi hangs in the background).

S: Yay! Daddi is going to learn something new! Daddi is going to learn something new too!

B: Wait, Daddi, I thought you knew everything about Everything!

D: No, my dear son, this is one thing I was never taught. Today, we are going to change all of that forever! The school we are going to go to today is called the Capital Markets.

S and B: Huh? The what, Daddi?

S: What the heck is that, Daddi?

D: The Capital Markets. Do you two ever wonder why you have such unusual, if not unique, first names? Do you ever wonder, Stocki, why your mom and I did not name you Shaniqua or Shanetta? And you, Bondi, why did we not name you Bahwi or Brommell? We did not do this because we knew there would eventually come a time when we would have to teach both of you about stocks and bonds. Thus, Stocki means "Stocks" and Bondi means "Bonds." Get it?

D: Capital means stocks and bonds which are assets. Assets are *good* things to own.

B: I still don't know what you are talking about, Daddi! What are you talking about?

S: Yeah, stocks and bonds? I just don't get it!

D: Quite frankly, we also knew we would have to teach ourselves about stocks and bonds, and then your mother died.

S: Yeah, and then Mommi died.

D: Okay, I know it is tough on you with her passing. But we, your mother and I, agreed that one day, I would take you two to the Capital Markets, whether she lived or died! So here we go! Off to the Capital Markets!

S: Is this like going to the vegetable market?

B: Or the meat market?

S: Or the supermarket?

B: Or the fish market?

D: Yes, quite frankly, it is! But better! Come on! The sooner you brush your teeth, get showered, and have your breakfast, the sooner we will ALL find out.

S: But what is Capital?

B: Yeah, what is Capital?

D: Hold your horses, and you will find out soon enough.

S: Wait, Daddi, I want to know now!

D: All I can say is that I want you, me, and Bondi someday to be RICH! Filthy rich!

S: Daddi, what is RICH?

D: Let me explain briefly, but I want you to get ready. Stocki, do you remember how you and your brother, Bondi, wanted your mom and me to buy you two shiny new bicycles, but we could not afford them? That we "had to 'wait until payday?'" Well, if we make regular visits to the Capital Markets—I mean the STOCK and BOND MARKETS—we can become RICH and not have to wait for payday as EVERY DAY IS PAYDAY! Capisce?

S: Capisce.

B: Capisce.

D: Your mother and I wanted each of you to play in the Capital Markets at the earliest possible age. Stocki and Bondi, you were both just babies then. Your mother—may God rest her glorious soul—and I know people who were in their forties and fifties who knew NOTHING about the Capital Markets. They spent all of their lives working at jobs, sometimes more than one, until they were in their sixties and seventies. Because they did not teach themselves about the Capital Markets while they were younger, they ended up poor. DON'T LET THAT BE YOU! I REFUSE TO LET THAT HAPPEN TO *MY* CHILDREN!

S and B (together): No, Daddi, we won't!

D: If I learn how to play well in the Capital Markets and teach you two to do the same, we can buy you ALL the toys, computers, books, and video games you want within reason since, after all, I do NOT wish to spoil you!

S and B: Yay! Yay! Yay! Daddi, Yay!

D: Are you showered and dressed yet?

S: Yes, Daddi!

B: Yes, sir!

D: Now go and eat your breakfast.

S and B (together): We're going to the Capital Markets! We are going to the Capital Markets!

B: But, Daddi, what are the Capital Markets?

BOOK #2: ENTER THE CAPITAL MARKETS

Come meet the new characters again:

- *Madame Capital Market, a.k.a. Ma'am (M), is a middle-aged Black woman. She is the home of Corporation #1, Corpi #1 (C#1), Corporation #2, Corpi #2 (C#2), and Corporation #3, Corpi #3 (C#3). Again, they do magical things for the right price!*

Daddi to Stocki and Bondi: There she is now! Hello, Madame Capital Market. Hello, Ma'am!

M: Hello, Mr. Daddi!

D: What are you selling today?

M: Actually, go to Corporation #1 (Corpi #1 or C#1) and find out what he is selling today.

D to S and B: On our way inside Ma'am's Capital Market, we are going to meet some very interesting people, people who can show us wonderful things and make us RICH! For example, here comes Corporation #1 or Corp #1 now.

S: Corpi #1? Get outta here! That is *not* a real name! That is a crazy name!

D: That is *his* name, young lady, I would be very careful if I were you! Your name is *Stocki*, and his name is *Corpi #1*. It is short for Corporation #1. He is a corporation. A corporation is somebody or something that issues STOCK to make things or offers services or both. I know you do not like it when people make fun of *your* name. Please show him the same courtesy.

S (doubtful): Like, what does he make?

D to Corp # 1: Good morning. Corpi #1, please tell my daughter what you make.

C#1: Good morning, family. Well, I make ice cream that does *not* melt in the springtime, summertime or any other time of the year.

S and B (together they do a sharp intake of breath): Huh?

S: Do you really?

C#1: Yes, I do.

S: You're right, it is not melting!

S: Daddi! Daddi! I, too, want to make unmelting ice cream!

C#1: You can if you give me money, and I can give you STOCK in Corp #1.

S: Daddi! Daddi! Corpi #1 used my name, Stocki!

D: Well, almost. What Corpi #1 wants to do is EXCHANGE your MONEY for STOCK. You give Corp #1 money from your purse. I slipped some money in there this morning without you looking. He will give you pieces of paper or computer transactions known as STOCKS. He will use that money to go back to his house and make more handheld non-melting ice cream machines.

S (still doubtful): Daddi, what do I get in EXCHANGE for MY MONEY? What?

D: You will OWN A PIECE OF PAPER OR A COMPUTER TRANSACTION FOR THE MACHINES THAT MAKE THE YEAR AROUND UNMELTING ICE CREAM. The more machines he makes, the more ice cream he sells, and the more money you will make, which is called a DIVIDEND. These are called CORPORATE PROFITS. Forget that for now. You are too young to understand that for now. Just consider it as MONEY that comes back to you. Stocki, with this EXCHANGE of MONEY for STOCK, you have become a STOCKHOLDER. Not only do you get dividends over time, but also, if your stock becomes more valuable, people will want to buy it. That means it is worth more! In other words, the more people that want your stock, the more valuable it becomes! You have to TRUST ME ON THIS. I will explain when you are, say, fifteen years young!

S: Okay, Daddi. I will wait.

B: Daddi, Daddi, what about me?

D: I gave you money too. It is in your wallet.

B: I see it, Daddi, I see it!

D: What C#1 wants to do with you is for you to LEND him some MONEY for a fixed period. He will give you BONDS in EXCHANGE for your MONEY. This BOND is also called an IOU. It means that he owes you money after a fixed period, like six months to a year. In exchange, from time to time, you will get MONEY back from Corpi #1 called INTEREST or LITTLE *i*. With this EXCHANGE of MONEY for BONDS, you have become a BONDHOLDER. In addition to receiving interest, you will get your money returned by Corpi #1 after the fixed life of the loan or if and when you SELL the bonds.

B: I like that, Daddi! Do I get lots and lots of INTEREST or a small amount of INTEREST?

D: That all depends. In a few minutes, you are going to meet *Ms. Fedi* or *Principal B* who works within the Madam Capital Market. It is up to her if you get a big or a small amount of INTEREST. Ma'am, what else do have to show us today?

M: Family, come and meet Corporation #2 (Corpi #2 or C#2). She has something really special to show you! Corpi #2, meet Mr. D and his children.

C#2: Hello, family! A Pleasure to meet you! Children, how would you like to walk on the walls or the ceiling of your home or anywhere else?

S and B make sharp intakes of breath: Huh?

C#2: I have made these special boots that let you walk on walls and on the ceiling anywhere you like!

S and B (together): Get outta here!

C#2: Let me show you! (C#2 puts on the boots and proceeds to walk on the walls and onto the ceiling!)

S and B: Wow! Wow!

B: Awesome!

C#2: You two can be the owner of the machines that make these boots if you buy my stocks and bonds.

S and B: Daddi, Daddi, we want to buy the machines that make those boots that let us walk on the walls and ceilings anywhere!

D: Okay! Okay! But who is doing what? Stocki, are you buying stocks? And, Bondi, are you buying bonds? *Please note the* big difference *between the two*! They are not the same!

S: I will keep with stocks!

B: Yeah, me too, Daddi, I will stick with bonds!

D: Please make up your mind. *Remember, there is a BIG DIFFERENCE between the two*! Stocki, you are GIVING MONEY to C#2. In exchange, your stocks will become more valuable if C#2 makes money. Later on, you can SELL your stocks for MORE THAN WHAT YOU PAID FOR THEM TODAY! You can also receive dividends, which I will explain when you get older. STOCKI, you are OWNING a PIECE of a corporation. In this case, you are now OWNING a PIECE of C#2. BONDI, you are LENDING MONEY to C#2 in exchange for interest.

D: Notice that corporations, INCLUDING BANKS, can issue both STOCKS and BONDS while GOVERNMENTS, FEDERAL, STATE, MUNICIPAL (or CITY) AND EVEN FOREIGN, DO NOT ISSUE STOCKS. IN MOST CASES, THEY CAN ONLY ISSUE BONDS. That is why you can ALWAYS OWN a PIECE OF A CORPORATION OR A BANK, BY BUYING THEIR STOCK, BUT YOU CANNOT OWN A PIECE OF A GOVERNMENT. Thus, you can ALWAYS LEND MONEY TO A CORPORATION, A BANK, OR TO A GOVERNMENT when they need to raise Capital. But, for the most part, you cannot GIVE GOVERNMENT MONEY in EXCHANGE for STOCK. Reach into your wallets, get out your money, and buy the stocks and bonds for the boot-making machines!

S and B: Y AY! Y AY!

S: So, C#2, here is my money. Give me my stocks! When will I start receiving my *DIVIDENDS*?

C#2 to S: Just as soon as we start selling the boots and making money!

S: Y AY!

C#2 to B: You, too, can make money by *lending* me money to make the boots to make the machines to make the boots to walk on the walls and onto the ceiling.

B: Yay, Daddi, I want the boots! I want the boots!

D: Wait, Bondi! Remember, you are LENDING MONEY TO C#2 to make the machines that make the boots that let you walk on the walls and onto the ceiling! In six months, she will pay your money back with INTEREST.

B: I get you, Daddi!

D: Come on, you two.

M: Okay, Mr. Daddi. I have just one more stop for you to make. Please come meet Corporation #3 (Corpi #3 or C#3).

Corpi #3: Hello, family!

Family: Hello.

C#3: I understand you bought stocks and bonds to buy machines that prevent ice cream from forever melting?

Family: Yes!

C#3: Also, you bought stocks and bonds to make machines that make boots that let you walk on the walls and onto the ceiling?

Family: Yes!

C3#: Well, I have a machine that is bigger and better than them all! How would you like to become *INVISIBLE*?

S and B: Whaaaaaat?

D: I agree! What?

C#3: That is what I said. Invisible! Please come over here. Here is my handheld invisible-making machine. I press a few buttons here and a few buttons there, and poof, I am invisible.

S and B: Daddi, Daddi, where did C#3 go?

D: That is the point. She made herself invisible!

S and B: We want her to come back!

S: Yeah. We want her to make us invisible too!

D: Madam Capital Market, please make C#3 come back!

M: Okay! (M Claps her hands and Corpi #3 reappears!)

C#3: Well! What do you think, kids?

B: I want to LEND money to C#3 that will make me invisible too! That way, when BULLIES WHO MAKE FUN OF MY NAME come along, I can hide from them and become invisible.

S: Yeah, me too. But I want to GIVE money to C#3 so that I, too, can hide from the BULLIES! C#3, do you make those invisible making machines?

C#3: Yes, I do, and no one else on the planet Earth makes these machines! No one! I own what is called a *PATENT* that prevents them from doing so! A patent is a piece of paper or a computer file issued by the United States Government that prevents them from doing so. Well, Stocki, here are your stocks! Well, Bondi, here are your bonds! Where is your cash?

S and B to Corpi #3: Here it is.

S: Daddi, I am tired.

B: Me too, Daddi.

D: I am kinda tired too! We had such a full day! You two are NOW proud stock and bondholders in C#1, C#2, and C#3. Let us say we try them out before we go on to our next adventure. Stocki, start making the ice cream.

S: Roger, Daddi.

D: Bondi, start putting on the boots so you can walk on the walls and onto the ceiling. Be careful that you don't fall out of them!

B: Roger, too, Daddi.

S: Daddi and Bondi, watch out as I make us all invisible!

B: Here we go. So long, WORLD!

D: So long!

S: So long!

B: Bye-bye!

    End of Book #2.

BOOK #3: ENTER THE DEFENDERS

Come, meet the latest characters again!

- *Mr. SECi, Principal A*; the Securities and Exchange Commission. He makes certain that Ma'am Capital Market and the Corpis do *not take advantage* of Daddi and his children, Stocki and Bondi.
- *Ms. Fedi, Principal B;* the Federal Reserve Bank. She makes certain that the Corpis *behave* with Stocki and Bondi by managing *Little i* or *Interest* in order to stabilize prices and the economy.

Mr. SECi, Principal A to Daddi, Stocki, and Bondi: Good day, family! I am Mr. SECi, Principal A in Madam Capital Market. I make certain that you and your children know what they are getting into BEFORE they give their money to the Corpis. You should make certain that your children GET A PIECE OF PAPER THAT TELLS THEM ALL ABOUT UNMELTING ICE CREAM, WALKING ON WALLS AND CEILINGS, AND BECOMING INVISIBLE. It is called a PROSPECTUS or a PROSPI. It tells THEM THAT THEY CAN BOTH MAKE AND *LOSE* MONEY by giving money to the Corpis. So next time, ask for a PROSPI *before* they invest.

D to Mr. SECi: We will.

Ms. Fedi, Principal B to Daddi, Stocki, and Bondi: Good day, family! I am Ms. Fedi, Principal B in Madam Capital Market. I am not a "bank" bank, like where you put money in and take money out. I manage something called the INTEREST RATE or *Little i*. Like toys, books, video games, computers, bread, eggs, milk, and meat, MONEY = A THING. There is no difference. The NAME of the COST OF MONEY is called INTEREST or *Little i*. INTEREST RATES, as they are called, RULE THE WORLD! When Corpi #1, Corpi #2, and Corpi #3 want to pay INTEREST, I, Ms. Fedi, want to make certain that THEY DO NOT ABUSE YOUR CHILDREN.

End of Book #3.

BOOK #4: ENTER EVERYTHING ELSE

Come meet the last set of characters again:

- *Riskis (R);* Risks. Stock and bond buying involves risks. That is what everybody needs to watch out for *before* investing.
- *Diversi (D);* Diversification. This, Diversi, is everybody's *best* friend. Stocki and Bondi must be mindful to *not* place all their eggs in one basket.
- *Evil Taxis (T);* Taxes. Those are the evil taxes that everybody hates, particularly on *April fifteenth of most years.*

Riski to Family: Hello, Family! BEWARE! When you BUY stocks and bonds, you are NOT putting money into a typical bank. That kind of bank money IS protected by the federal government. NOT SO when you buy stocks and bonds! These purchases involve R-I-S-K! Just like you can make money, you can also LOSE MONEY by buying stocks and bonds. Here is where I will let Diversi take over.

Diversi to Family: Hello, Family! When you buy stocks and bonds, make certain to buy more than one stock or more than one bond, which you have done. That is what is called a Big Word, which is called DIVERSIFICATION. That means not putting all of your eggs in one basket.

S: What? Daddi, what are they talking about?

B: What? I don't get this, Daddi!

D to S and B: Calm down! Let me explain. Diversi is simply saying, let us say that Corpi #1 may no longer be able to make the machines that make unmelting ice cream, and you lose money. But Corpi #2 can still make the machines that make magic boots and Corpi #3 can still make the machines that make us invisible. ALL IS NOT LOST. Just because you lost money with Corpi #1, you are good to go with your stock and bond purchases in Corpi #2 and Corpi #3 because they are still in business. That is what Diversi is talking about. You did NOT lose all your money, just some of it.

S: Oh, Daddi, I get it.

D to B: What about you, Bondi? Do you get it?

B to D: Yes, I do, Daddi. I think so. Just because one egg broke, the other two eggs are still whole because they were in separate baskets. Yeah, I get it!

D to S and B: Now we need to talk about something that EVERYBODY HATES, and that is EVIL TAXIS or TAXES.

Evil Taxis to Family: Hello, Family! No one wants to talk to me, but you must! It is the law. When you make money in Ma'am Capital Market with Corpi #1, Corpi #2, and Corpi #3, you have to GIVE *some* of that money BACK TO THE GOVERNMENT. Just some. Not all. That is called a TAX.

S to D: Huh? Daddi, what is he talking about? Give *my* money back? Why? It is MY MONEY! I want to KEEP MY MONEY. I don't want to give ANY OF IT BACK TO ANYONE!

B to D: Yeah, me neither! I want to KEEP ALL OF MY MONEY SINCE IT IS MINE!

D to S and B: Again, calm down! Let me explain. Do you remember when Grandma Lilli's house caught fire last year? And the fire trucks came and put the fire out? Remember?

S and B to D: Yes, Daddi.

D to S and B: Also, remember when I was robbed last year, and the police came by our house and took a report? And they caught the guy? Well, somebody has to PAY for the fire and police services. That's where your TAXES go. Without those taxes, Grandma's house would have surely burned down, and they never would have caught the bad guy.

S to D: Oh! I get it. So maybe taxes are not all that EVIL.

B: Yeah, Daddi, maybe taxes are a GOOD THING!

D to S and B: So, my sacred children, aren't you glad that you came to the Capital Markets today?

S: Yeah, Daddi, I want to be R-I-C-H!

B: Me too, Daddi, I want to be R-I-C-H too!

D to S and B: Lunch, anyone?

S and B to D: I'm starved!

D: Let us rock and roll! Children, say so long to Mr. Taxes, Mr. SECi, and Ms. Fedi.

S and B: So long, Mr. Taxes, Mr. SECi, and Ms. Fedi!

All: So long, Family! So glad we have met you today!

Family to All: So are we!

THE "i's" HAVE IT!

THE END.

Afterword

Dear families, thank you for *making* the time to read my sacred book. I hope you have all learned something new. If you have, I know that this will bode well for the future economic and generational wealth of you, your sacred children, and all people of African descent everywhere.

Going forward, with the help of God, I hope to create additional books that go deeper into the workings of the Capital Markets. Today, we have merely scratched the surface as it were. I wish to cover more investment issues and tools such as the economy, the various national and international stock markets and exchanges, the futures markets, short-selling, negative interest rates, the yield, the dollar, the Treasurys, the tax-free investing, the mutual funds, the money markets, bankers' acceptances, repurchase agreements, derivatives (that is tough one!), and so on. This subject of investing is *endless, complex,* and *extremely fascinating*—at least to me. I wish to break it down further for you, and I dare say for me!

Have a great and *profitable* day!

Paula Whitney Best, MA, JD

Resources

Investopedia. www.investopedia.com. The premier website for the educated investor.

The nightly business news of any major news network, cable news station, or streaming service.

NPR's Marketplace, 6:30 p.m. to 7:00 p.m. EST, on the air or streaming from NPR.org, provides a wrap-up of the important business news of the day.

CNBC—a major business news application.

Motley Fool. www.fool.com has been providing investing insights and financial advice to millions of people for over twenty-five years.

Robinhood. www.robinhood.com is a commission-free stock trading and investing application with tools to help shape your financial future.

About the Author

Paula Whitney Best, MA, JD, is an African-Caribbean American former corporation attorney admitted to practice law in the states of New York and Connecticut. They failed both bar examinations on the first try. Luckily, and with belief in themself this time, they passed both on the second try. Their undergraduate degree is in economics from Oberlin College. They hold a law or juris doctor degree (cum laude and a published member of the law review) from the Cardozo School of Law of Yeshiva University followed by a master's degree from New York University.

Their first "real" job after college was as an account executive with a mutual fund. After only five months there, they were promoted to training instructor for account executives. They were responsible for teaching the stock and bond market portions of the training. They did this for more than three years. Since then, they have covered these markets for more than forty years.

After law school, they went on to Wall Street uptown to an international corporate law firm for nearly two years. Then they chose to become a Manhattan Assistant District Attorney where they worked for nearly four years.

Completely astonished by the number of times they had inquired of pension-holding professionals of African descent who could not articulately distinguish between a stock and a bond, they wrote this book.

Printed in the USA
CPSIA information can be obtained
at www.ICGtesting.com
LVHW070018250924
791985LV00013B/110